LAUGHING MATTERS

HISTORICAL JOKES

Compiled by Pam Rosenberg
Illustrated by Patrick Girouard

Special thanks to Katie Cottrell for her assistance in compiling source materials.

Published in the United States of America by The Child's World®
PO Box 326, Chanhassen, MN 55317-0326
800-599-READ
www.childsworld.com

Acknowledgments
The Child's World®: Mary Berendes, Publishing Director

Editorial Directions, Inc.: E. Russell Primm, Editorial Director and Line Editor; Katie Marsico, Assistant Editor; Matthew Messbarger, Editorial Assistant; Susan Ashley, Proofreader

The Design Lab: Kathleen Petelinsek, Designer; Kari Thornborough, Page Production

Library of Congress Cataloging-in-Publication Data
Rosenberg, Pam.
  Historical jokes / compiled by Pam Rosenberg ; illustrated by Patrick Girouard.
      p. cm. — (Laughing matters)
  ISBN 1-59296-281-5 (library bound : alk. paper) 1. World history—Juvenile humor. 2. Riddles, Juvenile. I. Girouard, Patrick. II. Title. III. Series.
  PN6231.H47R67 2005
  818'.602—dc22   2004016863

What kind of lighting did Noah use for the ark? Floodlights.

What did Noah do to pass the time on the ark? He fished, but he didn't catch much because he only had two worms.

Teacher: In history, we have had the Stone Age and the Bronze Age. Can anyone name another age?
Patrick: The sausage.

Who was the world's greatest thief? Atlas, because he held up the whole world!

ANCIENT EGYPT

Why was the Egyptian girl worried?
Because her daddy was a mummy.

Where do mummies go swimming?
In the Dead Sea.

Why did the Egyptian mummy go to the resort hotel?
It needed to unwind.

Why was Cleopatra so negative?
Because she was the queen of denial.

Knock Knock.
Who's there?
Plato.
Plato who?
Plato fish and chips, please.

ANCIENT GREECE

Why did Socrates like the french fries?
Because they were made in ancient Greece.

ANCIENT ROME

First Roman soldier:
What time is it?
Second Roman soldier:
XX past VII.

What pastry wanted
to rule the world?
Attila the Bun.

What ancient people
traveled the most?
The Romans.

Why did Julius
Caesar buy crayons?
He wanted to
mark Antony.

CONQUISTADORES

Where did Montezuma go to school?
Az Tech.

Teacher: The Spanish explorers sailed around the world in a galleon.
Patrick: How many miles did they get to the galleon?

How did Columbus's men sleep on their ships?
With their eyes shut.

9

KINGS, QUEENS, AND OTHER NOBLE PERSONS

Why were the early days of history called the Dark Ages?
   Because there were so many knights.

What did the dragon say when he saw the knight in shining armor?
   Oh no. Not more canned food!

Why did the knight run around asking for a can opener?
   He had a bee in his suit of armor.

When a knight in shining armor was killed in battle, what sign was put on his grave?
   Rust in peace.

What would you get if you crossed the Hundred Years' War with the War of the Roses?
Very old flowers.

Who invented fractions?
Henry the Eighth.

What was the first thing Queen Elizabeth did upon ascending the throne?
Sat down.

Why did Robin Hood only steal from the rich?
Because the poor didn't have anything worth stealing!

What would you get if a famous French general stepped on a land mine?
Napoleon Blownapart.

What English king invented the fireplace?
Alfred the Grate.

Teacher: The early settlers had many hardships. Name one.

Matt: I know one. The wooden *Mayflower* was a hard ship.

If April showers bring May flowers, what do May flowers bring?
Pilgrims.

Why did the Pilgrims cross the Atlantic in the *Mayflower*?
It was too far to swim.

13

THE AMERICAN REVOLUTION

Who yelled, "Coming are the British"?
Paul Reverse.

What did they do at the Boston Tea Party?
I don't know.
I wasn't invited.

Teacher: Can you tell me what death is?
Russell: Patrick Henry's second choice.

Where was the Declaration of Independence signed?
At the bottom.

What did they wear at the Boston Tea Party?
T-shirts.

If George Washington were alive today, what would he be famous for? Old age.

Why was George Washington buried at Mount Vernon? Because he was dead.

Who succeeded the first president of the United States? The second one.

16

THE OLD WEST

Why did the pioneers cross the country in covered wagons?
They didn't want to wait 40 years for a train.

Who was the most feared student in the Old West?
Bully the Kid.

Did Native Americans hunt bear?
Not in the winter!

How do you make a strawberry shake?
Introduce it to Jesse James.

Who robbed stagecoaches and wore dirty clothes?
Messy James.

HONEST ABE

Father: When Lincoln was your age, he walked 10 miles to school.
Son: And when he was your age, he was president.

Teacher: Abraham Lincoln had a very tough childhood. He had to walk several miles to school each day.
Nicholas: Why didn't he get up earlier and catch the bus like everyone else?

Teacher: Anna, can you tell me about Lincoln's Gettysburg Address?
Anna: No, but I can call information and get the phone number.

THE 20TH CENTURY

When was the Great Depression?

The last time I got my report card.

Do you know the 35th president of the United States?

No, we were never introduced.

What would you get if Mickey Mantle married Betty Crocker?
Better batters.

ODDS AND ENDS

Mom: Why aren't you doing very well in history?
Jake: Because the teacher keeps asking about things that happened before I was born.

What do history teachers talk to each other about?
Old times, of course.

What is the fruitiest subject to study?
History, because it has so many dates.

23

About Patrick Girouard:

Patrick Girouard has been illustrating books for almost 15 years but still looks remarkably lifelike. He loves reading, movies, coffee, robots, a beautiful red-haired lady named Rita, and especially his sons, Marc and Max. Here's an interesting fact: A dog named Sam lives under his drawing board. You can visit him (Patrick, not Sam) at www.pgirouard.com.

About Pam Rosenberg:

Pam Rosenberg is a former junior high school teacher and corporate trainer. She currently works as an author, editor, and the mother of Sarah and Jake. She took on this project as a service to all her fellow parents of young children. At least now their kids will have lots of jokes to choose from when looking for the one they will tell their parents over and over and over again!